Make It HAPPEN

Solomon Dubner

PODCASTER

BY RYAN HUME

Lightswitch
LEARNING

150 East 52nd Street, Suite 32002
New York, NY 10022
www.lightswitchlearning.com

Educators and Librarians, for a variety of teaching resources, visit www.lightswitchlearning.com

Library of Congress Cataloging-in-Publication Data is available upon request.
Library of Congress Catalog Card Number pending

ISBN: 978-1-68265-580-1

2 3 4 5 6 7 8 9 10

Solomon Dubner by Ryan Hume

Edited by Lauren Dupuis-Perez
Book design by Sara Radka
The text of this book is set in Minion Pro Regular.

Printed in China

Image Credits

"If you want to be something, don't wait until you're an adult to do it. Do it now. It will only help you."

SOLOMON DUBNER

•   •   •

Make It! HAPPEN!

Skills for Success

Both searching for and then working toward a career can be challenging work. This recurring feature at the end of each chapter will help readers build toward career readiness. The "Make It Happen!" activity will tie relevant information from every chapter into ideas about career readiness. It will enable readers to more easily reach a variety of goals to ensure success in school and in the community.

Become an Announcer 15

Design a Podcast 23

Make a Study Plan 31

Prepare a Script 39

Tell a Story 47

Contents

Introduction 6

Early Life 8

First Steps of the Journey ... 16

Overcoming Obstacles 24

Teamwork 32

Current Career 40

Career Spotlights 48

Defining Moments 50

Depth of Knowledge 52

Create a Business Plan 53

Glossary 54

Read More 55

Internet Links 55

Bibliography 56

Index 56

Introduction

Solomon Dubner has always been interested in sports, but he wasn't always interested in soccer. It took a trip to England for him to see how universally exciting soccer really is. This new perspective led him down a road to discovery. He has now become one of the United States' youngest **experts** on international soccer through the **podcast** he created with his father called *Footy for Two*. Having overcome challenges in school due to a learning disability, Solomon has proven that following your passion can be a recipe for success.

In reading about Solomon, you will learn about his journey to becoming a happy kid. You will also discover that by working hard, being disciplined, and getting support from family members and others in the community, you too can develop passions that could turn into a fun and fulfilling career.

Solomon Dubner speaks to a large and diverse audience through his podcast, *Footy for Two*.

Soccer is now Solomon Dubner's greatest passion.

1 Early Life

Solomon's family has always been a big part of his life, going on adventures together and supporting one another.

Who is Solomon?

Solomon Dubner was born in 2000 in New York City. Solomon lives with his dad, mom, and younger sister, Anya. The Dubners are very close and enjoy each other's company. "We just talk a lot," Solomon says.

Sports have always been important to Solomon.

Ever since he was a young boy, Solomon has always enjoyed sports. He began playing American-style football, but when he was 13 years old he started to focus on playing soccer. Soccer is also called fútbol or footy in different parts of the world. Fútbol is the Spanish word for football. People in England call it footy for short. Footy also refers to the ball itself. Both American football and fútbol are team sports that involve the matching of two teams against one another. While American football players throw and catch the ball using their hands, fútbol or soccer players use only their feet, heads, and bodies to move the ball across the field. In soccer, only the goalie can use their hands to catch the ball.

DID YOU KNOW?

Solomon and his dad are both big Pittsburgh Steelers football fans.

Solomon's Family

Solomon's dad, Stephen, is a **journalist**. Stephen has been writing ever since he was a child. He started publishing articles in magazines, such as *Highlights,* when he was 14. In college, he started a rock band. Eventually Stephen decided to focus on his writing. He was an editor and writer at *The New York Times* newspaper and won many awards for his writing. When a writing assignment brought him to Chicago and he met economist Steven Levitt, his life changed forever. Economists study how people make and sell things and also how people buy and use those things. They are also interested in watching where money ends up in different societies. Does it only go into the hands of the rich? Or does it get spread around to different people? Together Steven Levitt and Stephen Dubner wrote a book called *Freakonomics*, which uses ideas about economics to uncover interesting, weird, and unexpected patterns in the world. For example, some unique topics of the book include how shoes change the way feet work, and the effects of good parenting on education.

Solomon's dad, Stephen, has always been a huge support.

Make It Happen!

CRASH COURSE IN SPORTS PODCASTING

Apple Podcasts: a podcast directory and app for listening to podcasts through iTunes

broadcast: to send out (signals, programs, etc.) by radio, television, or the internet

defense: the group of players on a team who try to stop an opponent from scoring

download: to move or copy (a file, program, etc.) from a usually larger computer system to another computer or device

episode: a television show, radio show, etc., that is one part of a series

FC: Football Club

offense: the group of players on a team who try to score points or goals against an opponent

podcast: a program (such as a music or news program) that is like a radio or television show but that is downloaded over the internet

The book was a big hit and quickly became an international bestseller. Stephen learned to use **social media** to continue to grow the *Freakonomics* **fan base**. He hosts a podcast called *Freakonomics Radio*, which is available on **Apple Podcasts** and other **apps**. The podcast is also **broadcast** around the country on National Public Radio (NPR) stations. *Freakonomics Radio* is now downloaded more than eight million times each month. That's twice the population of Los Angeles.

Solomon has grown up with *Freakonomics* in his life.

The Dubner family likes to have fun. Anya and Stephen enjoy adventures like apple picking.

Inspired by Family

Solomon's mother, Ellen Binder, is a photographer. Before Solomon was born, Ellen moved to Russia to take photographs. She lived there for a number of years before returning to New York City. Her work has appeared in magazines and newspapers around the world. She has traveled to many places to take photographs, including Afghanistan and Cuba. She has won awards for her photographs. She has also taught photography at a variety of schools around New York City. Solomon has learned from his mother that no matter what kind of art you make, it's a great way to communicate with different people. Building on the lessons he learned from his mother, Solomon discovered for himself how helpful the internet can be. It can even help you find new jobs based on your artwork.

Solomon's younger sister, Anya, is now 15 and interested in fashion. Solomon and his sister have seen their parents follow their passions and turn them into successful and fascinating careers. Stephen and Ellen are examples of what happens when you find something you are good at and commit to hard work. They have shown that if you take **initiative** and **collaborate** with others, success is possible. Still, it might not come easy. Solomon has experienced some of his own setbacks. Thankfully, he has always had his family's support.

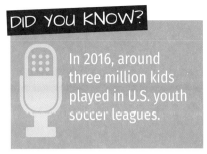
History of Soccer

The first known game that involved kicking a ball was called Cuju. It originated in China more than two thousand years ago. Other early ball-kicking games came from ancient Greece and Rome. Roman soldiers used to kick a ball around as part of their military exercises. These balls used to be filled with hair! More than a thousand years ago, the Romans brought the first ball-kicking game to England. Soccer, or football, remains incredibly popular there today.

What we now know as soccer started in England in 1863. It developed out of a similar game called rugby. Rugby can be described as a cross between soccer and American-style football. Players use their hands and their feet to move the ball, and they can tackle each other. It took many years for the rules of today's soccer to be agreed upon.

Soccer as Community

For Solomon, soccer is about more than just exercise, fun, and competition. He has found that through the sport, he has made many connections and plenty of new friends. "American soccer fans are a community because there aren't that many of us, though that number is steadily and rapidly growing," he said. "When you meet another American soccer fan, you have an instant connection that you wouldn't in Europe. I have plenty of friends who I have nothing in common with . . . except for the fact that we love soccer." A passion for the game creates a special bond between its fans.

It was this passion and his exposure to podcasts that led Solomon toward starting a podcast of his own. Solomon's initiative and supportive family helped him begin this exciting journey. His ability to connect with strangers over a common interest has made him a success.

> "When you meet another American soccer fan, you have an instant connection that you wouldn't in Europe. I have plenty of friends who I have nothing in common with . . . except for the fact that we love soccer."
>
> **SOLOMON DUBNER**

DID YOU KNOW?

There are more than 90 youth soccer clubs in New York City. The largest club, the Manhattan Soccer Club, serves more than 800 families.

Make It HAPPEN!

Become an Announcer

Professional soccer is the fastest-growing sport in the United States today. Major league teams, or football clubs, hire various people for different jobs. One way to get involved in the sport you love is to get into broadcasting. Many teams hire announcers to describe the action of a game to eager fans over the radio, TV, and online.

You can start practicing at home! All you need is a television set and a computer.

- Tune in to your favorite sporting event.
- Try to tell the story of the action without listening to or reading about the event.
- Use the computer to look up information on your favorite players or teams.
- Use the information to keep talking in between the plays.
- You can even use a microphone to record yourself talking.
- Listen to your recording after the game and make notes about how to improve.

How did you do? Did you miss any big plays? Did you call everything correctly?

2

First Steps of the Journey

Solomon enjoys playing soccer anywhere, including London, England, at age 9.

Solomon's trip to London had a big impact on his life.

A Meaningful Trip

Solomon first recognized the importance of soccer when he went to England with his family in 2010. The trip was at the same time as the World Cup, which is the largest soccer tournament in the world. It takes place once every four years. Though the tournament was thousands of miles away, in South Africa, Solomon noticed that everyone in England loved it.

"That's the only thing that matters in the country for a few weeks," Solomon recalled. "Everyone was following it fervently. Everywhere we went, soccer was everywhere—everybody was watching it, talking about it, reading about it."

Solomon had never followed soccer before then. He didn't realize how important it was to people all over the world. "Before I went on that trip, I didn't like soccer," he said.

DID YOU KNOW?

The first World Cup took place in Uruguay in 1930. In 2018, the World Cup will be in Russia.

Discovering Soccer

One day in England, Solomon went out to an Italian restaurant with his sister and a family friend. A World Cup game was on the TV. "We were watching England vs Algeria and I remember this game was important to the U.S., who I was rooting for even though I didn't like soccer," Solomon said. "Everyone thought England was going to blow Algeria out of the water." Even though the room was cheering for England, Solomon **predicted** that the final score

To become an international soccer expert, Solomon has had to travel around the world.

would be a draw. This means no goals are scored for either team. "Everyone thought it was going to [be] England by [a score of] five–zero. And at the end when it was zero–zero, everyone is looking at this ten-year-old American like he's a genius when really I knew nothing," he continued.

After that moment, Solomon fell in love with fútbol. He started playing on a team in middle school in 2013. Solomon currently plays in four different leagues: indoors in the winter and outdoors in the spring and fall. He often plays midfielder, an **offensive** position.

DID YOU KNOW?

Brazil holds the record for the most World Cup titles, having won five times.

Soccer Positions

In soccer, or fútbol, there are 11 people on the field for each team. Each teammate plays a certain position. Each player has a specific job. Some protect the goal and try to keep the other team from scoring. Others attack the other team's goal and try to score as many points as possible.

defender

defender

midfielder

midfielder

midfielder

striker

striker

defender

defender

goalkeeper

Connecting with Others

Solomon has always enjoyed sports and participating in fun runs for charity.

Solomon has always been interested in sports. In addition to playing fútbol and American football, he also competed in track and field. Through sports, Solomon found a way to connect with people.

Like fútbol, podcasting is also a great way to reach others with similar interests. Podcasting first became popular in 2004, when Apple's iTunes store began offering podcasts for download.

Radio shows are broadcast over the **airwaves** and are monitored by the Federal Communications Commission (FCC). There are fewer restrictions in podcasting. Today, there are many kid-friendly and kid-led podcasts. More are made each year. Listeners can find podcasts on every possible topic, including comedy, history, and music, as well as soccer and other sports.

Solomon soon saw his dad doing the *Freakonomics* podcast every week and growing his audience to millions of listeners. "He started his journalism career when he was fourteen," Solomon mentioned. "I was first published when I was thirteen, though I'm not trying to compete," he joked.

DID YOU KNOW?

The word "podcast" comes from two separate words: "pod" from Apple's iPod, and "cast" from the word "broadcast."

> **66** [My dad] started his journalism career when he was fourteen. I was first published when I was thirteen, though I'm not trying to compete. **99**
>
> SOLOMON DUBNER

Solomon has applied the same work ethic he has seen from his parents to his podcast today.

FIFA and the World Cup

FIFA stands for the Fédération Internationale de Football Association. It is the organization in charge of international football. Today FIFA represents 211 different nations from around the world. The large-scale World Cup tournament happens every four years.

The U.S. women's team has competed in every Women's World Cup. They earned a medal in each appearance and have won the championship three times. They are the 2015 Women's World Cup Champions. The best result for the U.S. men's team came in 1930, when they came in third place. Between 1950 and 1990, they did not participate in the Cup.

In 2014, nearly four million people attended World Cup matches in Brazil. More than one billion people watched the final match between Germany and Argentina.

Footy for Two

Solomon started his podcast, *Footy for Two*, in March of 2016. The original idea was for Solomon to explain soccer to his dad, who doesn't know that much about the sport. Solomon had to work hard to bring in his own listeners. While podcasts are quite popular, it is still challenging to keep steady listeners. Due to Solomon's wit, charm, and knowledge of the game, *Footy for Two* has become a hit. Within the show's first year, Solomon and his dad made 50 **episodes**.

> "It's never too late to start. And don't be afraid to be different."
>
> **SOLOMON DUBNER**

Footy for Two reviews games, discusses FIFA rules, and makes predictions for future matches. Solomon also discusses anything having to do with **FC** Barcelona, his favorite fútbol club. "All sports can bring people together," Solomon said. "But with soccer, I feel that the average fan is more passionate. You are born into loving a club." Across the world, these fans are known for their extreme passion for their favorite football clubs.

"It's never too late to start," Solomon said about podcasting. "And don't be afraid to be different. I know everybody says that, and it's easy to shrug it off, but it's true." Being different has given Solomon an edge in the podcasting world. No other soccer podcast is exactly like Solomon's.

DID YOU KNOW?

In 2005, George W. Bush became the first U.S. president in history to make a podcast. Every president since has continued to use podcasts to talk to the nation.

Make It! HAPPEN!

Design a Podcast

Is there a subject that you feel passionate about? Music? Animals? Baseball? A podcast is a great way to share your interests with other people.

Some things you need to decide before you get started:

- Narrow down your idea. You'll need to find your niche, or focus. Are there any other podcasts that cover the same idea?

- Pick a catchy name for your podcast. You'll want a name that clearly describes what your podcast is about.

- Design your **brand**. Create a logo that will help give your podcast a brand people will remember.

- Decide what equipment and software you will need to record and edit your podcast. There are many free videos on the internet which can help you decide on equipment and teach you how to edit audio.

How are you keeping your podcast voice unique, like Solomon suggests?

3

Overcoming Obstacles

School started out being a challenge, but with the right help Solomon was able to succeed.

ADHD

ADHD can make paying attention difficult, but Solomon has always loved books and reading.

Despite his success, Solomon has had setbacks in school and life that he has had to overcome. "I was just a little scrawny, shy kid and I wasn't very comfortable coming out of my shell," he said. School was hard for Solomon at first. He would later understand that being different was a good thing. But at first, it brought many different challenges.

Solomon found the school he started at did not let him **thrive**. "You had to learn in one single way," he said. "And I wasn't able to learn that way. I have ADHD and math-based learning disabilities." Solomon felt his teachers targeted him for being different.

ADHD stands for Attention Deficit Hyperactivity Disorder. Students with ADHD often have trouble sitting still for long periods of time and paying attention in class. In some cases, they can also have trouble controlling their feelings and can act out. ADHD is most often noticed in children or young adults.

DID YOU KNOW?

Many famous athletes have been diagnosed with ADHD. Olympic swimmer Michael Phelps and basketball legend Michael Jordan both have ADHD.

School Challenges

Some days were really hard at school as Solomon was ignored by his teachers. He grew quiet and removed as his teachers continued to not **engage** him. "I would cry in my room most nights," Solomon remembered. "It was hard." His mom and dad always told him, "It will get better. Keep working hard. Believe in yourself."

Eventually Solomon's parents moved him to a different school. "I went to another school for kids with learning disabilities, where I thrived and made great friends and became comfortable being myself," he said. He was reluctant to attend the new school at first. "Change is always scary, especially when you are young," Solomon added.

Once Solomon got the attention he needed, he thrived.

DID YOU KNOW?

Since 2011, 6.8 million children in the U.S. ages 4–17 have been diagnosed with ADHD. ADHD affects 11 percent of all school-aged children.

For the first two days, he didn't like his new school. Everything was different. "It was scary, but then I made friends, joined student council, the soccer team, everything," he said. His new school turned out to be the kind of environment where being different was celebrated, not looked down upon. Solomon got more attention in the small class settings. Many students with ADHD do much better in smaller classrooms. Solomon was finally getting the support he needed to learn and thrive at school.

ADHD diagnosis in the United States

ADHD is very common all across the United States. See below for a map showing the percentage of people who are diagnosed in each state.

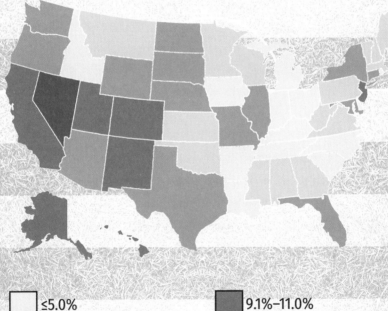

≤5.0%	9.1%–11.0%
5.1%–7.0%	≥11.1%
7.1%–9.0%	

Becoming a leader in track and field gave Solomon confidence.

Gaining Confidence

Solomon also gained confidence through sports at his new school, including track and field and playing on the soccer team. Solomon recalled that in the past in group projects, he would have sat back and observed. In his new environment, he took a leadership role. One day during a track meet, Solomon took the lead in a race. His whole school, about two hundred students, began chanting his name from the stands. "Even as I was running, and giving everything to win that race, I was thinking, 'This is where I belong.'"

Taking on team-leadership roles and jumping into sports competitions helped Solomon come out of his shell and find his voice. This confidence would later become important to his success as a podcaster. Listeners enjoy Solomon's podcast because he is different and able to express his own opinions about life and soccer.

"I loved my middle school," he said. "But I knew I needed to go somewhere that would be academically challenging so I'd be able to get into the kind of college I want to attend." By the time he finished middle school, Solomon was a much different person than just a few years earlier. He became a self-confident, social, dedicated student athlete.

Solomon's parents made sure he was able to transition easily when he moved to a new school.

Success in Sports and Life

The leadership and collaboration skills learned while playing sports can impact future success. Myrone Rolle is the perfect example of this. He is a former National Football League (NFL) player. He played football in college for Florida State and was drafted by the Tennessee Titans in 2010. He is now studying to be a brain surgeon at Harvard Medical School. Rolle told CNN in 2017, "Football has done so much for me, given me friends, family, given me life lessons that now I can use in the operating room or just as a leader."

Finding His Stride

Due to his newfound confidence, Solomon immediately fit in at his new high school. Even still, transitioning into a new school can always be a challenge. "It was tough at first, going from a thirty-six-kid grade to an eighty-kid grade, but it was really nice and I fit in really quickly. The transition was hard not being with my best friends every day, but I made new friends and now I fit in really, really well."

Podcasting is a family affair. Even the dog is included.

With the *Footy for Two* podcast, Solomon and Stephen have mostly avoided major errors. There has really only been one big problem that Solomon remembers. "I was recording an interview with my friend Julian," Solomon recalled. "I didn't realize that when we were recording the battery on the recorder died and we lost the whole episode! We eventually rerecorded, but it was really annoying."

DID YOU KNOW?

People ages 12–24 are the second-largest age group listening to podcasts right now. They make up 27 percent of all listeners. The largest age group are people 25–54 years old.

Make It HAPPEN!

Make a Study Plan

You can develop good study habits by being prepared and planning ahead. Just like training for a sport, the more prepared you are before a test, the more you will succeed. Think of your current study habits. What are three ways you can be even more prepared than you are now? Some examples include:

- Set up a new calendar for each new school year.
- Ask your teachers if you can use a recording app to capture school lessons.
- Set up a homework routine.
- Collaborate with friends to review notes and share ideas on how to study.
- Try to sit at the front of the class, ask your teachers questions, and let them know if you are having any difficulties.

Apply and then revisit these techniques after you take a test or quiz. Do you feel like you succeeded? What helped and what didn't?

4

Teamwork

Traveling with his family has given Solomon the unique worldview he brings to podcasting.

The Power of Family

At just 16 years old, Solomon Dubner has already found some great success by launching his own podcast. However, no one gets to the top without overcoming challenges and receiving help from friends, family, and teachers.

No one has made more of an impact on Solomon's career than his dad, Stephen. Even though he had been watching his dad do his own podcast for years, Solomon didn't know how to get started with his own. "I didn't know how to write out a script for a show," Solomon said. Stephen not only assists in the recording process and serves as a regular guest, he also helps expand the show's **outreach**. This means attempting to widen its audience. "He has a big platform," Solomon said of his dad's eight-million-plus listeners. "Most of our listeners come from *Freakonomics*."

Family support is one of the main reasons Solomon has succeeded.

Solomon and his dad record their podcast every week at their dining room table. Solomon crafts the talking points for each show by using a **template**, which helps him outline what they'll discuss. "Some of the shows are scripted," Solomon went on, "while others aren't." They work around the family's schedule so they don't get in the way of his mom and younger sister. "Sometimes you'll hear a door opening and closing, but it's not that professional so we don't really care," he added.

DID YOU KNOW?

Forty-two million Americans listen to podcasts at least once a week. That is 13 percent of the total U.S. population!

Sharing Interests

Stephen also helps Solomon avoid feeling discouraged. An example of this came when Solomon believed that his podcast would grow an audience faster. "He said to me, 'People are generally taking a half hour out of their day to listen to you talk about soccer—two or three thousand people. That's a lot of people,'" Solomon said of his dad. It seems their podcasting relationship is very helpful. Stephen taught Solomon a lot about writing and recording. In addition, Stephen learned a lot about soccer from his son. "He gave me the Steelers and I gave him Barcelona," Solomon said.

The rest of his family is important to Solomon, too. "We are a very loud family in a very loving way," Solomon said. His mom, Ellen, has taught him some important lessons. "My mom has always taught me to not take 'no' as an answer, except, of course, when it's from her," he jokes. His younger sister, Anya, is even credited with coming up with the name of his podcast, *Footy for Two*. "She came up with the name," Solomon mentions in an early episode of his podcast. "I think she wants to **copyright** it!"

Solomon and his sister Anya keep each other company at family events.

Make It Happen!

Another important person in Solomon's life is Simon Kuper, one of Solomon's idols and the co-author of *Soccernomics*. He is one of the top soccer journalists and works for the *Financial Times* newspaper. Kuper was born in Uganda to South African parents and has been writing about soccer for many years. The book *Soccernomics* is based off the idea of *Freakonomics*. Solomon got the chance to interview Kuper for his podcast. "I just picked his brain," Solomon said. "And we have an episode of that." Kuper is one of the reasons Solomon wants to go into soccer journalism or broadcasting after he graduates from college.

Simon Kuper is a Life and Arts columnist at the *Financial Times* newspaper.

Solomon credits his soccer coach, Travis, with helping him improve his game. "I met Travis on my birthday a few years ago shopping at the soccer store near my apartment," Solomon recalled. "Since then, we've played together a lot. He's made me a much better player and taught me a lot about the game. He's also been on the show a bunch and we're collaborating on some projects together."

DID YOU KNOW?

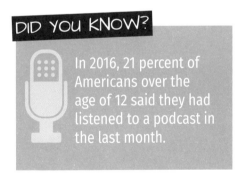

In 2016, 21 percent of Americans over the age of 12 said they had listened to a podcast in the last month.

The Podcasting Community

Podcasts are a fun way for kids to practice public speaking and research, and to develop creativity. Solomon is a great example of what can happen when passion and technology meet. There are many podcasts for kids and by kids available on the internet. Podcasting is made up of many different communities. If you are interested in starting your own podcast or starting to listen to some, these are some good places to start.

EAR SNACKS

Produced by "Andrew & Polly," this music-centered podcast interviews children to get their perspectives on different topics. It also features a soundtrack.

SPARE THE ROCK, SPOIL THE CHILD

This podcast, from Bill Childs, highlights indie music for kids and features Bill's children, Ella and Liam.

BUT WHY

This podcast, from Jane Lindholm and Melody Bodette, features questions asked by children. The children are usually recorded by their parents, and the audio is played and discussed on the show. The hosts have touched upon a number of different topics.

BRAINS ON

From MPR News and Southern California Public Radio, *Brains On* features a different science lesson every week. The neat thing? It's hosted by "kid scientists." The show also touches on a bunch of different topics.

PODCAST KID

Hosted by "Jenna and her Dad," the show covers all the subjects related to younger kids. This includes making friends or moving out of town.

Friends Make a Difference

Another inspiring force in Solomon's life is his friend Nick Crawford. Crawford is a competitive hockey player with hopes of playing professionally. They met in middle school. Crawford once told him, "You've got to use those [speaking] skills to reach people and tell them what you think."

Nick and Solomon went to a soccer match together at Yankee Stadium in New York City.

Although he had difficulties learning at school when he was young, there have since been two teachers in Solomon's life who have helped him on his journey. Solomon credits his English and Math teacher, Ms. Kalogeros, for helping him regain his confidence. "She took me aside for lessons ahead of what the class was doing and really taught me to believe in myself," he said. Another teacher, Mr. Maloney, crossed paths with Solomon when he was in the seventh grade. "[Mr. Maloney] was a massive soccer fan," Solomon remembered. "He taught me to keep fighting in life after he got in a big car crash and kept living successfully and happily."

DID YOU KNOW?

In 2015, only half of Americans age 12 or older said they were familiar with the term "podcasting." So, while podcasts are growing, people are still somewhat unfamiliar with them.

Make It HAPPEN!

Prepare a Script

While not every episode of *Footy for Two* is preplanned, it is a good idea to write a script for your podcast episode before you hit the record button. Recording a podcast could take about 20 or 30 minutes. Writing out a script will help you organize your thoughts and get through every subject you want to cover. Follow these steps to prepare your own script:

- On a sheet of paper or spreadsheet, make a list of subjects in the order that you want to discuss them in your podcast.

- If you are featuring a guest, write out a series of questions that you want to ask them. You may also want to write out a brief introduction, including important information that explains to your listeners why you are having this guest on your show.

- Write down any facts, statistics, dates, or quotes that you may need to use during your podcast. You want to have all this information available so that you don't have to pause during your recording session.

After you record, revisit the script. Did you hit all your points? Did you add new topics while recording? How effective was your podcast preparation?

5

Current Career

Solomon has conducted several interviews in New York City for his podcast.

Next Steps

Solomon is now looking ahead to the next chapter of his life. By collaborating with his family, friends, and teachers, he has already created a popular soccer podcast that reaches thousands of people around the world every week. He learned how to turn his passion for the game of fútbol into an entertaining and educational show. He uses his humor and knowledge of the sport to improve his podcast every week.

Solomon has been able to watch his favorite teams abroad. He went to a Spain vs Croatia match while in France.

By working hard and learning to **network** and collaborate, Solomon has met many people working in the fútbol world. Today, he is fast becoming known as an expert. On earning the respect of other soccer fans, Solomon said, "It feels nice that they don't care about my age; that they don't write me off because of it . . . Because a lot of people would. It's nice to know that they are giving me a chance and listening to me talk."

DID YOU KNOW?

The Dun Cow Football Club was established in 2014 and plays in the Greenhouse Shrewsbury and District Sunday Football League. The team is known as "The Cow," and Stephen Dubner is its honorary president.

Solomon continued, "The great thing about this era is that anyone who has something to say can say it and get it out to people."

Connecting with people from all over the world is a big part of why Solomon loves soccer and his podcast.

Fans of Footy for Two

Every day, Solomon receives emails from his growing fan base. "I get them from all kinds of people," he recalled. "I got one from an eight-year-old, one from an eleven-year-old in Newcastle, England, and my favorite one was from a 67-year-old woman from Vermont, who used to live in New York." The woman had recently been in a terrible car accident. "She is recovering," Solomon clarified, "but she has been getting back into soccer and following it again and she found my show and sent me paragraph after paragraph asking me to explain things to her."

DID YOU KNOW?

Solomon's favorite soccer player is Lionel Messi, the Argentina-born forward who plays for FC Barcelona and is widely considered one of the best players in the world.

At matches, it is easy to make new friends when you are all cheering for the same team.

Solomon's love for soccer has been felt around the world, and not just because of his podcast. In one case, Solomon's dad agreed to help out an English soccer league in need of funding. This came after a 15-year-old named Alex Simpson emailed Solomon's dad asking for help. Stephen agreed, financially helping the Dun Cow FC. *Freakonomics Radio* still sponsors Dun Cow. Because soccer is such a global phenomenon, Solomon has been able to connect with others around the globe through his love of soccer.

Top 40 Sports Podcasts According to Podbay

1	*30 for 30 Podcasts*
2	*Pardon my Take*
3	*The Ringer NBA Show*
4	*Louisville Talk Radio 1080*
5	*I Am Rapaport*
6	*The Bill Simmons Podcast*
7	*The Herd with Colin Cowherd*
8	*The Full 48*
9	*First Take*
10	*The Lowe Post*

Solomon is part of the FC Barcelona fan club in New York City. They watch games together and celebrate wins as a group.

Career Aspirations

Solomon is hoping to turn his podcast into a career in journalism or broadcasting and hopes to keep podcasting through college. He plans to cover both soccer and **politics**. Politics is another one of his passions. He has already **interned** for his local New York City councilwoman.

Podcasting is also a great way to get experience for TV and radio broadcasting jobs. Podcasts are inexpensive to make and available to millions of people at the click of a button. This means that anyone can become a podcaster and create a large body of work to showcase their personality and interests. This is a good way to start out in the TV or radio industry.

Even as he begins to think about his future, Solomon has watched his audience for *Footy for Two* continue to grow. Now, with more than three thousand hits per episode, many people have noticed the program, including Penya FC Barcelona NYC. A *penya* is a Spanish word that describes an official group of fans that support a chosen fútbol club. Barcelona is Solomon's favorite club. With around five hundred members, Penya FC Barcelona NYC is "the biggest Barcelona supporters group outside of Spain," Solomon said. This local chapter of Barcelona fans in New York City has asked Solomon to host a new podcast specifically for their organization. Solomon is hoping to start this new challenge soon.

Grant Baciocco

There are many different types of podcasts. Not all podcasts are non-fiction. Some focus on telling stories. Grant Baciocco has created a podcast that is all about adventure. *Saturday Morning Theatre* is a series of serials. This means it takes several episodes for a story to complete. Some of the stories are mysteries or westerns or superhero tales. All of them are unique and are voiced by a host of different actors. Baciocco also created the podcast *The Radio Adventures of Dr. Floyd*. This podcast follows an evil genius who is always trying to battle against his nemesis, Dr. Steve. One of the best parts of podcasting is that even when a series is complete, people can still discover them for the first time in **archives**. *The Radio Adventures of Dr. Floyd* is over, which means listeners can now enjoy the entire podcast without waiting.

Solomon continues to be a fun, happy, and outgoing person.

Moving Toward the Future

With the confidence that he found by working hard and following his passions, it's likely that Solomon will figure out a way to continue to be successful. He has already learned how to manage his ADHD. He has become a dedicated student and athlete. He has made many friends around the world and started a popular podcast. Solomon will soon be applying to colleges, where he plans to study journalism, history, and political science.

His emerging leadership skills in putting together a show, and cultural skills in reaching out to people across the globe, continue to grow as the podcast evolves.

DID YOU KNOW?

Penya FC Barcelona NYC's mission statement reads: "we represent the city and our commitment to introduce fútbol, not only as a sport, but also as a catalyst for a greater good."

Make It HAPPEN!

Tell a Story

Many jobs in entertainment, including podcasting, are centered around storytelling. Storytelling can take many forms. Sometimes podcasting is personal, where people talk about their life experiences. Sometimes it is topical. This means the show is focused on a specific topic, like Solomon's show. Other podcasts entertain listeners with made-up stories. What story would you like to tell? Practice storytelling with a friend.

- Talk about recent events that have happened in your life.
- Was there something funny or scary or sad that you would like to share?
- After discussing with a friend, write down your story.
- Once you are done, read them to each other.

Be open to giving feedback. What worked in the story? What would you have liked to hear more of?

Career Spotlights

Solomon may be young, but he has already experienced so much. He has created and maintained his own podcast, built and kept a solid base of listeners, and overcome a learning disability. Below are some of his important career moments.

First Article Online

In 2013, Solomon publishes his first article online at the age of 13. He becomes an active blogger about his passion for soccer.

World Soccer Talk

In 2014, Solomon writes for the popular website *World Soccer Talk*, previewing games for the new season.

Footy For Two

Solomon's first episode publishes on March 10, 2016. This is the episode that started *Footy for Two*, a free-wheeling conversation between father and son.

"Simon Kuper Interview"

This is Solomon's personal favorite episode of *Footy for Two*, where he gets a chance to interview one of his idols, the soccer journalist Simon Kuper.

"Will Grigg Is on Fire!"

This June 29, 2016 episode of *Footy for Two* has had the most listeners to date.

Defining Moments

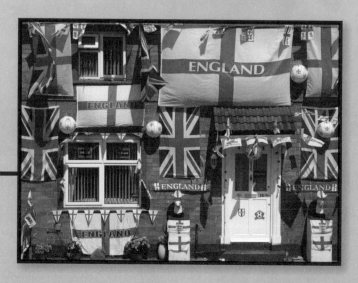

During a trip to England, Solomon is first exposed to the manic popularity of fútbol culture. With the FIFA World Cup going on in South Africa, the whole country of England is obsessed. Solomon becomes obsessed as well.

2010

Solomon has trouble in school. Having been diagnosed with ADHD, he struggles in class as his teachers don't engage him.

2010

Solomon and his family travel to Barcelona, Spain. Solomon attends his first professional soccer match. It is between his favorite club, FC Barcelona, and their local rivals, RCD Espanyol. Solomon is surprised by how passionate and intense the rivalry between the two clubs is.

2012

2013

Solomon joins his middle school's soccer team.

2016

Solomon launches his podcast *Footy for Two* with his father, Stephen Dubner. They record 50 episodes of the podcast that first year.

2017

Solomon works hard at school to improve his grades and initiates a plan to go to college.

Depth of Knowledge

1   Explain how Solomon's parents and their careers have inspired and influenced him. What has been their greatest impact? Has their influence changed over the years? Use examples from the text to support your answer.

2   Describe how traveling abroad shaped Solomon's opinion of the world. Analyze the importance of collaborating with people in other cities and countries to his current work.

3   Develop a list of skills, such as initiative and resiliency, that are important for an **entrepreneur** like Solomon. Describe how each of these skills helps a person to reach their goals.

4   Write an argumentative essay on this statement: All students should be taught the same way. Do you agree or disagree? Support your argument using clear reasoning. Draw on relevant evidence from this text and other reliable sources.

5   Choose a person with a successful career in your community who you would like to interview. What questions would you ask them? Research the individual—their personal life and their career. During the course of your research, continue to develop your list of interview questions.

Create a Business Plan

Create a business plan for the podcast you've created from the Make It Happen! features in this book. The finished document will map out how to turn your podcast into a thriving business.

- a group of 3-4 students
- paper and pencils
- internet access

1 Communicate with your group members to answer these questions: What are the goals of your business? What makes your podcast different? What is your target market? Using your answers, write a company description.

2 Research other podcasts on the internet. Analyze the strengths of your competitors and the reasons for their success.

3 Decide how your business will be organized and assign responsibilities to group members.

4 Establish a marketing plan. Use creative thinking to decide how to sell your podcast to advertisers and subscribers.

5 Make financial projections. This can include a three- to six-month plan for your expected costs and income.

6 Collaborate to write a few paragraphs for each section. Finish by reviewing your work and writing a concise summary, which will go at the beginning of your business plan.

Glossary

airwaves *(noun)* the signals used to broadcast radio and television programs (pg. 20)

app *(noun)* a computer program that performs a special function (pg. 11)

Apple Podcasts *(noun)* a directory and app for listening to podcasts through iTunes (pg. 11)

archive *(noun)* a place where older documents are stored (pg. 45)

brand *(noun)* a category of products that are all made by a particular company and all have a particular name (pg. 23)

catalyst *(noun)* a person or event that quickly causes change or action (pg. 46)

collaborate *(verb)* to work with another person or group in order to achieve or do something (pg. 13)

copyright *(verb)* to obtain the legal right to be the only one to reproduce, publish, and sell a certain piece of media for a set period of time (pg. 34)

engage *(verb)* to cause someone to take part in something (pg. 26)

entrepreneur *(noun)* a person who starts a new business (pg. 52)

expert *(noun)* a person who has special skill or knowledge relating to a particular subject (pg. 6)

fan base *(noun)* a group of people who like a specific sports team, musician, etc. (pg. 11)

initiative *(noun)* the determination to learn new things and improve skill levels on your own; the ability to get things done (pg. 13)

intern *(verb)* to work for a period of time at a job in order to get experience (pg. 44)

journalist *(noun)* the activity or job of collecting, writing, and editing news stories for newspapers, magazines, television, the internet, or radio (pg. 10)

network *(verb)* to talk with people whose jobs are similar to yours especially for business opportunities or advice (pg. 41)

outreach *(noun)* the activity or process of bringing information or services to people (pg. 33)

politics *(noun)* the work or job of people, such as elected officials, who are part of a government (pg. 44)

predict *(verb)* to say that something will or might happen in the future (pg. 18)

social media *(noun)* forms of electronic communication (such as websites) through which people create online communities to share information, ideas, personal messages, etc. (pg. 11)

template *(noun)* something that is used as an example of how to do, make, or achieve something (pg. 33)

thrive *(verb)* to grow or develop successfully (pg. 25)

Read More

Buckley, James, Jr. *Sports Media Relations.* Broomall, Pa.: Mason Crest, 2016.

Burdick, Debra E. *Mindfulness for Teens with ADHD: A Skill-Building Workbook to Help You Focus and Succeed.* Oakland, Calif.: Instant Help, 2017

Luke, Andrew. *Soccer.* Inside the World of Sports. Broomall, Pa.: Mason Crest, 2017.

Morgan, Alex. *Breakaway: Beyond the Goal.* New York: Simon & Schuster, 2015.

Simons, Rae. *Sports Math.* Broomall, Pa.: Mason Crest, 2014.

St. John, Warren. *Outcasts United: The Story of a Refugee Soccer Team That Changed a Town.* New York: Delacorte Press, 2012.

Internet Links

http://freakonomics.com/footyfortwo/

https://solomondubner.wordpress.com/

https://www.eofire.com/top-7-strategies-how-to-grow-your-podcast/

https://www.teenlife.com/blogs/10-alternative-careers-sports

http://kidshealth.org/en/teens/learning-disabilities.html

https://www.additudemag.com/slideshows/famous-people-with-adhd/

Bibliography

"Simon Kuper Interview." *Footy for Two.* Freakonomics, LLC, 18 June 2016. Web. 27 June 2017.

"About ADHD." *CHADD—The National Resource on ADHD.* Children and Adults with Attention-Deficit/Hyperactivity Disorder (CHADD), 2017. Web. 27 June 2017.

"Ellen Binder, Stephen Dubner." *The New York Times.* The New York Times, 12 Sept. 1998. Web. 27 June 2017.

Quirk, Vanessa. "Podcasting: A Brief History." *Guide to Podcasting.* Tow Center for Digital Journalism, 7 Dec. 2015 Web. 27 June 2017.

Shearer, Elisa. "Audio and Podcasting Fact Sheet." *Pew Research Center's Journalism Project.* Pew Research Center, 16 June 2017. Web. 27 June 2017.

"Stephen J. Dubner." *WNYC.* New York Public Radio, 2017. Web. 27 June 2017.

Index

Attention Deficit Hyperactivity Disorder (ADHD) 25, 26, 27, 46, 50

Binder, Ellen 9, 12, 13, 26, 29, 32, 33, 34

collaborate 13, 31, 35, 41, 52, 53

Crawford, Nick 38

Dubner, Anya 9, 12, 13, 32, 34

Dubner, Stephen 9, 10, 11, 12, 13, 20, 21, 22, 26, 30, 32, 33, 34, 41, 43, 51

Dun Cow FC 41, 43

England 6, 9, 13, 16, 17, 18, 42, 50

FC Barcelona 22, 34, 42, 44, 45, 46, 50

Fédération Internationale de Football Association (FIFA) 21, 22, 50

Footy for Two 6, 22, 30, 34, 39, 42, 45, 49, 51

Freakonomics 10, 11, 20, 33, 35, 43

initiative 13, 14, 51, 52

Ms. Kalogeros 38

Kuper, Simon 35, 49

Mr. Maloney 38

New York City 9, 12, 14, 38, 40, 44, 45

Soccernomics 35

World Cup 17, 18, 21, 50